THE RIDING AIDS

THE RIDING AIDS

BASIC TERMS OF HARMONIOUS COMMUNICATION

BETWEEN RIDER AND HORSE

CLARISSA L. BUSCH

CADMOS
EQUESTRIAN

A note on headwear

The photographs in this book are of highly experienced riders and were composed specifically to illustrate particular points in the text concerning the various aids. In a small number of photographs, the riders are shown wearing no riding hat, as was their personal choice. This is not to be encouraged and it is assumed that most riders will prefer at all times to wear appropriate safety headwear when riding.

Copyright of German edition © 2000 by Cadmos Verlag
Copyright of this edition © 2002/2006 by Cadmos Equestrian
Translated by Konstanze Allsopp
Layout: Ravenstein Brain Pool
Photos without reference: Peter Prohn
Print: Landesverlag, Linz
All rights are reserved.
Reprint or storage in electronic media
only with written permission from the publisher.
Printed in Austria.
ISBN 3-86127-905-3

DRESSAGE MOVEMENTS AND EXERCISES

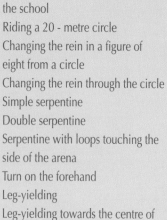

THE RIDER'S AIDS

The aids are the language between horse and rider. The signals of the rider's aids allow the horse and rider to communicate with each other. This communication is not - as one might think at first - unilaterally directed from the rider to the horse. The horse has the choice of accepting the aids willingly or fighting against them, thereby signalling to the rider what the latter is doing wrong.

The term "aids" is used for the invisible co-ordination between the unity of rider and horse. In the ideal case, the rider should only have to think of the execution of the task for the horse to react promptly and correctly. However, it takes a long time to attain this goal. One pre-requisite is that the rider and horse have both learned this language of the aids.

In principle, an inexperienced rider should always learn the aids from a well-trained horse, and a young horse should learn the aids from an experienced rider, in order to eliminate the many misunderstandings which would

A correct seat, upright and relaxed, invisible aids and the horse moving in harmony with its rider.

occur otherwise, and which would have a negative effect on the training of horse and rider in the future.

It is often assumed that the horse will automatically understand correctly applied aids and will react to them in text book fashion. This, however, does not usually happen because the situation described in equitation manuals is normally based on a carefully trained and highly gifted horse. In real life, most horses which are not ridden in high-performance competitions will only experience a brief and not always perfect training period. Riding school horses, in particular, often learn the aids under different riders and in a great variety of ways. Such horses tend to learn that they will only have to accept what the rider seriously intends to enforce. The horse will simply ignore vague and poorly defined aids which are not applied with the necessary willpower.

Independent of this, the physical predisposition of horses varies greatly. Some lessons or paces will be easier to perform, others a horse will find harder to achieve. This also needs to be taken into account when applying the aids to the horse. For the rider, these considerations mean that he will have to co-ordinate his aids with the training status of the horse. The aids are always given in the same way, but their intensity and method of application depend to a large degree on the schooling status of the horse. The rider will only develop a feeling for this after years of riding many different horses. A less experienced rider should therefore ask his riding instructor for helpful hints.

A correct seat is the first prerequisite for the rider to be able to apply the aids correctly. Flexible aids which are independent of the rider's and horse's motion can only be applied if the rider has a balanced and relaxed seat. The balance, in particular, is extremely important for the execution of the aids.

The number one rule is to find and maintain one's balance on the horse's back. Under no circumstances should the rider have to hold on or even have the feeling that he needs to hold on to something. He should always balance his weight so it lies directly above the horse's centre of gravity. Thus, the rider only maintains his seat on the horse by always sitting directly vertically above the horse's spine.

When riding turns, the rider must ensure that he sits in the middle. That way, he will not have to cling onto the horse with his hands or legs. Another sign of lack of balance is lifting one's hands, as the rider tries to compensate his lack of balance with his hands, instead of maintaining it solely with his upper body. The seat needs to be so balanced that the rider is capable of holding his hands absolutely still and using only conscious restraining and yielding rein aids. He must prevent his hands following the movement of his body at all costs. Similarly the rider's legs must never thump against the horse's sides following the rider's motion. They need to be used to drive the horse in a controlled manner. In order to achieve this balance, the initial training of the rider should include extensive lungeing lessons. Even when the rider has reached a more advanced stage, it will not harm him to occasionally take a lungeing lesson to correct his seat. In this context, however, the important thing is not a one-off correc-

Lungeing lessons: safety for beginners, intensive correction of the seat for advanced riders.

tion but the constant work of the rider concerning his or her seat. During the lungeing lesson, the instructor will only point out the rider's mistakes to him. A visible improvement of the seat will only occur if the rider continuously checks and corrects his seat himself whenever he is on a horse.

THE WEIGHT AIDS

Weight is the most important but at the same time the least active aid of the rider. Simply by sitting upright and thereby pressing down with his weight onto the horse's spine, is the horse encouraged to move forwards. This makes it very important that the rider sits straight and upright, without hollowing his back, hunching up his shoulders and curving his spine outwards. The weight aids are transferred to the horse's back via the seat bones. If the rider is sitting relaxed and without tension, he should be able to feel how his seat bones press down on the saddle (they are located more or less in the centre of each buttock). Many riders press their weight away from the horse by tensing up their seat muscles. It is important to relax these muscles and really let the entire weight fall down until you can feel the pressure

The rider gives way in the outer hip joint, pulls up the inner shoulder and holds her head in a crooked position. This upsets the balance for both horse and rider.

against the seat bones. This relaxation of the muscles is just as important when in motion.

There are unilateral and bilateral weight aids. When moving forward at the walk or trot, the rider must use bilateral weight aids. He is sitting vertically over the centre of the horse and both seat bones press down on the sad-

dle with equal weight. In all curves, during the canter and for all lateral work, the rider uses unilateral weight aids. In this case, the rider transfers the weight to the inside of the bent horse. This automatically relieves the outside of the horse. The rider should make sure that he does not give with the hip, thus thrusting it outwards,

The rider correctly shifts her centre of balance inwards during the curve on the circle line without giving with the outer hip.

because he is trying to bring his upper body more to one side. The shifting of the weight should be carried out solely by moving the outer, restraining leg back and thereby increasing the load on the inner hip.

When performing the rein-back and riding in the forward seat, both sides of the horse are relieved of the burden of the weight aids. This means that the buttocks remain in touch with the saddle but the two seat bones no longer apply any pressure on the back of the horse. The forward seat has to be learned, in particular, for riding out on hacks or across country and for jumping, in order to be able to relieve the horse's back. In this position, the influence of the weight aids occurs via the thighs which rest against the saddle. These act either as forward-driving or restraining aids.

Giving in the hip joint (i.e. bending in the hip) is a serious fault which, once it has become a habit, is very difficult to correct and overcome. It will make life difficult for the rider in all future lessons, because the horse will become increasingly difficult on the respective side, due to the incorrect weight influence. This can even lead to uneven steps and serious problems of balance once the muscles of the horse have developed unevenly due to the unilateral burden of the rider's weight. If possible, you should always take the chance to ride

When the rider stretches his position in the saddle, the well-schooled horse will collect itself together, its impulsion becoming more pronounced - the effect of the mysterious bracing of the back.
Photo: Kruck

towards a mirror and check whether you are sitting straight on the horse or whether your hip joints are folded to one side. This fault can be seen best at the trot or canter. For this purpose, the riding instructor should inspect the rider's seat from the front and back. If the fault has become established, it needs to be eliminated immediately. To do this the rider needs to lift the shoulder, which will be lower due to the bent hips, in an exaggerated fashion to correct the fault and pull the other shoulder down. At the same time he must check whether the hip has slid to one side of the saddle. The back centre of the rider's seat should be in line with the middle of the saddle.

Bracing the Back

In addition to the more or less passive weight influence through placing it on the seat bones, we have the more active weight aid of bracing the back. In order to be able to harmonise the motion of the horse, the rider needs to tension and relax the muscles of his lower back and pelvis. Usually this occurs automatically in motion, as the rider adapts to the swinging motion of the horse's back and achieves a deep seat in the saddle. In more advanced equitation, the rider should however pay conscious attention to the influence of the spine. The relaxed forward-upward swinging of the middle part of the rider (the hip area of the rider) with the motion of the horse, is a prerequisite for a harmonious movement with the horse. The basic requirement for this is elasticity of the hips. During the canter, it is usually natural for the rider to swing forward in the hip. During the trot, the rider often sits more stiffly. However, the rider must swing forward-upward with the motion of the horse in this pace as well as in the walk. Usually, it should be sufficient with corresponding fine-tuning of the aids, to increase the bracing of the back in order to ride the horse forwards with more impulsion. At the same time the restraining seat with a stretched upper body should encourage the horse to hold the tempo. You will be able to practise increasingly this fine-tuning with the horse by trying to ride faster and slower and even change the pace with weight aids only, and use the rein and leg aids less and less. At the same time, the horse can learn to turn to the right or to the left purely in response to the unilateral weight aid.

To begin with, the rein aid will be used to assist the learning process, later the horse will react exclusively to the weight aid.

You can practise this at all paces, for example, on the circle. By placing increased weight on the inner side of the saddle (the right side on the right rein, the left side on the left rein) and at the same time using the outside leg more actively, the horse is encouraged to make the circle smaller. By placing more weight on the outside and using the inside leg increasingly, the horse is asked to enlarge the circle again. This exercise is particularly useful at the canter, as it also improves the straightness of the horse.

THE LEG AIDS

The leg aids are applied via the entire leg of the rider resting against the body of the horse. When using the leg aids you should ensure that these are applied from top to bottom. The horse is also driven forwards by the rider in the region of the upper thigh. The lower leg (calf) and the heels are tensed and relaxed against the horse's side in rhythm with the motion of the horse. If you are riding a sensitive horse, the leg pressure is applied almost automatically through the swinging motion without additional effort of the muscles. If the horse reacts less sensitively, the rider will actively increase the pressure of the legs. In any case, however, the aid needs to be followed by a relaxation of the muscles of the legs. Keeping up the pressure continuously is wrong. The leg aids are applied in

A balanced seat is the pre-requisite for correct leg aids. The lower leg on the girth drives the horse forward and/or encourages the horse to bend around it. In motion, the leg "breathes"" at the horse's side.

rhythm with the motion because the rider can only convey an impulse for the horse to move forwards at the exact moment at which the horse lifts up the appropriate hind leg. The rider needs to take care to acquire a feeling for the lifting of the leg on each side at all paces and to tense the corresponding leg muscles at that exact same moment.

The leg aids also differentiate between bilateral and unilateral driving signals. Just as with the weight aids, bilateral leg aids are applied when the horse moves forwards in a straight line, and unilateral aids are applied when the horse is moving in a curve. In this case, the outer leg acts as a restraining aid. The forward-driving leg aid is applied at the girth, whereby

The restraining leg, one hand's width behind the girth, acts as a restraint or as a driving aid for lateral movements.

the front edge of the rider's lower leg or riding boot is aligned with the rear edge of the girth. The restraining leg is placed a hand's width behind the forward-driving leg and prevents the horse's hindquarters from swinging out of line. Depending on the degree of restriction, this leg lies more or less passively against the horse's side.

In addition, we have the sideways driving leg aid for lateral movements, also applied one hand's width behind the saddle girth. Unlike the restraining leg aid, however, the sideways driving leg remains active at all times. It induces the horse to place its hind leg on the same side sideways underneath the body instead of straight forwards. The rider needs to take note whether

The upright closed fist around the rein allows a soft connection to the horse's mouth. Reins and lower arm to the elbow should be a straight line. Check this occasionally in the mirror, if you have the opportunity!

his leg aid gets through successfully and whether the horse really steps sideways. If it does not do this, or not to a sufficient degree, the aid must be increased in intensity for a short time. Naturally, lateral leg aids can only be applied unilaterally. The opposite outer leg acts as a restraining aid to prevent the horse's shoulder from swinging out, or as a forward-driving aid to maintain the forwards movement and impulsion. Any backward movement in lateral work is incorrect.

THE REIN AIDS

The restraining, backward rein aids should always be subordinated. You may only restrain the horse with the reins to the same degree that you have created impulsion and engagement of the hindquarters of the horse with the forward aids. The rider must always counteract the usual inclination of doing too much with the hands and using the legs and seat too little, to ride the horse forwards. The restraining rein aids need to be applied in small doses and very carefully in order to retain the sensitivity of the horse's mouth and in order not to provoke any resistance of the horse, whereby the rider is bound to lose. If a horse is ridden correctly, the rider maintains light contact with the horse's mouth via the reins.

The rider cannot enforce the horse's acceptance of the bit through the action of his hands. It is the result of the co-ordination of the driving and restraining aids. The seat and leg aids are predominant, not the rein aids!

In this context, you must ensure that the reins remain in steady contact with the horse's mouth, like a rubber band, and not hang slackly. This is largely a matter for the rider's hands, which need to remain steady, even when the rider is swinging to the motion of the horse. They must never interfere with the progress of the horse's motion. Depending on the degree of schooling of the horse, restraining rein aids will have to be given repeatedly.

If the horse does not react to light aids, such as shortening of the rein by pressing on the ring finger (squeezing the fist together, as if squeezing out a sponge), the next stage is a slight turning in of the fists holding the reins. Pulling back with the arms should be

avoided as this will always provoke the horse to evade the aids by pressing down its back and thus preventing any trusting contact between the rider's hands and the receptive horse's mouth. The bit should always act on the lower jaw of the horse and not pull at the corners of the mouth.

The restraining rein aids may only be applied for a short time and always need to be followed by a relaxing of the reins. Keeping a constant restraining contact with the reins is the wrong way. Shortening the rein unilaterally occurs in turning corners, bilaterally when the horse is straight. In turns, the rider helps the horse maintain a certain position to the left or right by unilateral shortening of the rein. Nev-

Pulling rein: the front of the horse's face is behind the vertical, it "walks on its head", does not place its hindlegs under its body to carry the weight and tenses up in the back muscles. This is aggravated by an incorrect seat of the rider with the weight resting on the upper thighs.

The bilateral giving rein aids encourage the horse to stretch itself forward. The horse continues to accept and maintain contact with the bit and the horse's mouth is approximately level with the point of shoulder, showing a clearly stretched neck posture.

er shorten the rein to such an extent that the horse is bent further in the neck than the first two to three cervical vertebrae. In this position the rider can see the respective inner corner of the horse's eye. He must never bend the horse to such an extent that the entire neck of the horse is bent sideways. Unfortunately, this fault is very common and causes the horse to swing out with its hindquarters. In order to introduce the position, the outside rein is lengthened as far as the inside rein is shortened. In this bent position both reins again maintain an elastic contact with the horse's mouth. The inside rein should only ask for a very slight bend and should only be shortened again, if the horse tries to turn its head away from this position too strongly.

CO-ORDINATION OF THE AIDS

Correct execution of the individual aid is not sufficient in itself. Rather, correct co-ordination of all aids is the important factor. Really good riding only begins once the rider has learned to use his aids together in such a way that he can encourage the horse to work in complete relaxation and acceptance of the rider without any resistance. The most important thing is the intensity of the individual aids. In the course of its training, the horse should learn to react to the lightest possible, invisible aids. The rider can achieve this through a conscious light application of the aids, which are intensified for a short time, if the horse does not react to the lighter aid. Once the horse does

react the aids are lightened again immediately. Rough aids deaden the horse's reaction in the long run and the rider will have to use increasingly more force or intense aids in order to get the horse to work with the rider. Counteract this development by always remembering to start off with very light aids.

THE HALF-HALT

Half-halts are often incorrectly termed as a slight pulling on the reins. The half-halt however is certainly not a rein aid but instead a short-term co-ordination of all aids. It is the only correct way of using the restraining rein aid: only in combination with increased contact with the lower leg and seat bones. Half-halts are used in a variety of situations.

When applying a half-halt, the rider stretches his body for a moment and balances his upper body vertically above his pelvis - like bricks which are placed on top of each other (bracing of the spine). Often this stretching is sufficient to encourage the horse to place his hind legs further under the body and collect himself together. At the same time, the lower legs of the rider increase their contact with the horse's sides and the rider's hands restrain the movement of the rein for a moment. This motion will encourage a well-ridden horse to come back from a working trot to a collected trot without losing rhythm during the transition, which could occur if the rider were to pull on the reins.

In transitions from a faster to a slower pace, the back aid must be applied

Invisible half-halts are applied as a preparation for the transition from the trot to the walk.

The rider stretches his upper body and braces his spine, which encourages the horse to transfer more of its weight onto its hind-hand.

... and changes into a rhythmic walk without losing the gentle contact with the rider's hand.

The full halt is prepared by applying half-halts. The aim is the correct halt with the weight evenly distributed on all four legs. Any corrections must always be made by walking forwards.

slightly more strongly, but at the same time lead the horse gently back into the new pace. When applying the half-halt, the rider must always make sure to apply it for only a short moment, even if the horse has not yet carried out the required reaction. In this case, the half-halts are repeated until the horse is ready to be collected and taken up.

The rider uses the half-halt continuously, to ensure that the horse accepts the bit and maintains contact at all times, to help it find the correct position and bend, to regulate the tempo, to improve the posture, to introduce lessons, to draw its attention to a jump, and on many other occasions. They are the most important communication means between horse and rider. Therefore, it is very important that they are carried out correctly.

THE FULL HALT

The full halt always means a transition to the halt. It always consists of a combination of several half-halts. The rider prepares the full halt by applying several half-halts until the horse comes to a stop.

If the rider simply pulls on the reins, the horse will evade the rider's aids and brake suddenly, with its weight tipping onto the forehand, instead of placing its hind legs further under its body and coming to a balanced halt.

If the rein aid is too forceful, the horse will fall onto the forehand at the full halt. It is more important to give with the reins than to pull at them.

THE RIDER'S AIDS ON THE MOVING HORSE

Soft acceptance of the bit by the horse and distinct expansion of the horse's frame combined with a non-restraining rein and correct positioning of the legs are the pre-requisites for the correct dressage walk.

AT THE WALK

It is relatively easy to sit correctly at the walk, as the horse moves without bouncing. However, the rider should take care at this pace to gently go with the horse's motion with his middle position, in other words the hip region, thereby encouraging the horse to walk forwards with impulsion. When walking out on a hack, the rider should take note of his seat.

Outdoors, most riders move with the motion of the horse with sufficient drive, because the horse is moving forwards with more impulsion. The driving power should not, however, be exaggerated, as this would cause the horse to go with hasty, short steps. The horse should stride out, place its feet calmly and with elevation. The calmy more the horse strides out, the longer its steps become, and the overall elevation and forward motion are improved.

Soft acceptance by the horse of the bit and distinct expansion of the horse's frame, combined with a non-restrain-

ing rein and correct positioning of the legs, are the prerequisites for the dressage walk.

The legs rest evenly at the horse's sides and press on the right and left alternately. If the rider lets his legs hang completely relaxed, he will feel how they alternately fall on their own against the horse's sides. This is the correct rhythm which effectively occurs on its own through the contraction and stretching of the horse's sides when it is moving. Initially, the rider can also control his aids to create impulsion by taking note of the picking up of the horse's front hoofs. He will use the driving aid at the precise moment when the front leg on the same side is moving back (i.e. is placed on the ground before it is picked up again), because the corresponding hind leg will be lifted directly following this. The aids to create impulsion, of course, support the movement of the hind legs. Forceful leg aids should be avoided as this can cause the horse to lose its rhythm, which constitutes a grave fault.

At the walk, the horse needs to be given optimum freedom of the neck. The horse's neck must be completely relaxed and stretched out at the walk. The horse does not have a working walk, but only a medium walk, which always requires a stretching of the horse's frame. Many riders, especially beginners, tend to ask for increased collection at the walk, strengthening the contact with the horse's mouth in order to improve the horse's acceptance of the bit, or because they are unable to put the horse on the bit at the trot or canter. We would seriously warn against this. By tightening the horse at the walk, the horse will very easily

fall into a rack-like rhythm which is very difficult to correct.

At the walk, the rider's hands and arms go with the natural movements of the horse's head and neck. This can even lead to the rider stretching his arms out completely to give the horse optimum freedom of its neck. Nonetheless, contact with the horse's mouth is maintained constantly even with the longer rein.

AT THE TROT

Rising Trot

The rider should stand up in the stirrups as little as possible and merely let the swinging motion of the horse lift him up. It is sufficient if the seat-depending on the impulsion of the horse-lifts only a few centimetres out of the saddle. It is wrong to actively push up the body out of the saddle. When sitting down again, the rider gently checks the motion of his weight with the legs supported by the stirrups, and carefully slides into the saddle. He will remain seated for a moment with a relaxed hip and braced back, before letting the horse lift him gently out of the saddle again. At the rising trot, the rider drives the horse forwards with his weight and legs when he is sitting down. At the moment when he is sliding into the saddle, he simultaneously closes both his lower legs against the horse's sides and pushes them backwards and downwards at the same time as far as possible, without however, pushing the heels away from the horse. The driving leg aids occur from the thigh in the direction of the heel. The rider closes

Rising trot on the right hind leg: when the left front leg moves forward, the rider lets the horse lift her a few centimetres out of the saddle.

When sitting down, the rider closes the thighs, knees and calves against the horse's sides and, in addition, uses the weight aid of his seat to drive the horse forwards. The gentle contact to the horse's mouth is maintained throughout.

his thighs, knees, calves and the heels every time he sits down. The weight aids are transferred to the horse's back via the seat bones. As a rule, the swinging motion with which the rider sits down in the saddle is sufficient to drive the horse forwards. The rider should take care not to sit either on the front part of the upper thighs (cleft seat) or on the back of the buttocks (lounging seat). At the moment of sitting down, the weight of the rider sits squarely and correctly on the triangle of seat bones and pelvic bone.

The arms and hands maintain gentle contact with the horse's mouth, whereby the line between elbow, hands, reins and horse's mouth remains straight. The rising and sitting motion of the upper body is merely compensated through a change of the angle of the elbow joint. Lifting up the hands when rising in the saddle, as can be observed frequently, counts as a fault.

Sitting Trot

At the sitting trot, the main aim is for the middle position of the rider to swing with the motion of the horse. If the rider has learned to smoothly adapt to the movements of the horse, he can start to push the hip forwards, "going with the horse's motion", in order to encourage the horse to lengthen the strides of its hind legs under its body. However, the rider needs to make sure not to use muscle force incorrectly for this aid, thus losing his relaxed seat. The secret is the elastic tension of the body. The term itself is almost an oxymoron and it is very difficult to explain how the rider's body must remain soft and flexible on the one hand, while yet

The moving of the middle position of the rider with the motion of the horse must not be confused with the common "pushings" forwards with the seat and spine. The elastic tension of the body of the rider which allows the horse to move forwards with impulsion and relaxed upright posture, is the result of years and decades of practice.

driving the horse forward with a light tensioning, on the other. For this to be successful, the rider needs extensive schooling and concentration which, however, will most certainly be worth the effort, as it is an essential prerequisite for all types of riding. Once the rider is experienced enough to be able to hold and drive the horse forward with his seat and back, he will immediately feel the difference. It conveys a special feeling of control of the horse with the help of minimal aids.

At the sitting trot, the legs don't drive the horse forwards every second stride, as they do at the rising trot, but with each lifting diagonal pair of legs instead. For this purpose, the rider's lower legs rest evenly at the horse's side with relaxed knees and are pressed against the horse in rhythm with the movement of the horse. Clinging on with the lower legs is wrong. The

intensity of the pressure of the calves right up to the short light nudge against the horse's side (only however in the rhythm of the movement) is dependent on the engagement of the horse in its forward impulsion.

As a general rule, the rider should drive the horse forwards with as little effort as possible, in order to teach it to react sensitively to the lightest aids. If the horse does not react to the light aids, the aids are intensified until a reaction occurs. Then immediately revert back to the light aids. The rider needs to observe at all times how well or badly the horse accepts his aids and adapt the application of his aids to this. At the sitting trot the hands should remain as steady as possible. This requires flexibility of the shoulder and elbow joints, which have to cushion the swinging motion of the horse in such a way that the lower part of the

The canter is a pace which is ridden with the horse bent to the inside. The rider increases the weight on the inside seat bone, which drives the horse forwards.

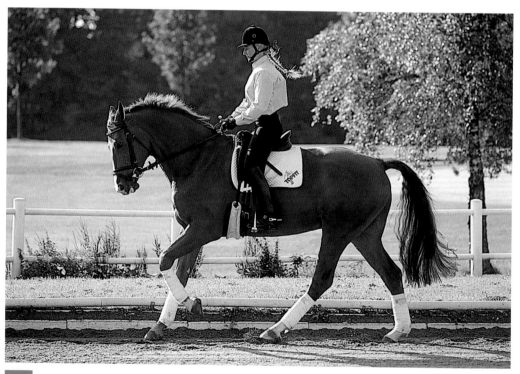

arms and the hands of the rider remain steady, independent of the movement. A swinging motion of the hands with the motion of the horse is wrong. Rein aids should only be given when necessary and in a controlled manner.

If the arms flutter about excessively, the rider can always squeeze his fists together, as if he was squeezing a sponge, as this will cause the muscles of his lower arms to tense and enable him to keep his hands steadier than if the lower arms and wrists are limp.

AT THE CANTER

The canter is a pace which is ridden with the horse bent to the inside. For this purpose the rider increases the weight on his inside seat bone and releases the outer seat bone at the same time. The relaxed weight of the rider is applied predominantly on the inner seat bone in the saddle to drive the horse forwards, but without sliding around in the saddle. The rider sits as if rooted to the saddle and "pushes" the horse's back in the direction of the inner corner of the horse's mouth with his inside hip. During the entire canter stride, the hip must move forwards with the movement and must not merely indicate the canter stride. At the same time, the rider's upper body stays upright and stretched. The outer shoulder must not slump back. The forward movement of the motion is carried out solely by the hips, not as it is often seen by the shoulders. Here, the rider has the feeling that his upper body falls backwards at each stride at the canter.

To increase the impulsion of the horse, the rider does not drive forwards with more force but rather pushes the

The canter has four phases - in each phase the rider remains sitting in the saddle, deep and supple.

The rider sits in a stretched posture with the legs resting well against the horse's sides. Her hands gently follow the movement of the horse. Photo: Busch

The inner lower leg creates the impulsion for each stride at the canter as if the horse starts to canter at every stride. Photo: Busch

At the canter, the horse is correctly on the bit and sensitive to the aids. However, the rider's position of the lower leg and her hollowed-out back need correcting.

rhythm forward, increasing the speed of the tempo and the application of the aids. However, the rider always needs to make sure that the strides at the canter are as long and rounded as possible, so that in the moment of suspension the legs of the horse remain in free suspension as long as possible. Short and rapid canter strides should be avoided.

The inner leg rests on the girth in a forward driving position and creates the impulsion for each new stride, as if the horse starts to canter at each stride. The calf presses in a relaxed manner against the horse's side in time. The outer leg lies behind the girth to act as a restraint. This prevents the horse from swinging out with its hindquarters. At unfenced

corners it is applied more actively than when the horse is riding on the outer track of a school, where the fence is a natural barrier. The intensity is dependent on the engagement and impulsion of the horse. Normally, a slight pressure of the leg against the horse's side suffices. If the horse threatens to fall back into a trot, a short nudging may be required to increase the impulsion at the canter once more.

The rein aids keep the horse on a slight bend to the inside. The inner rein is shortened until the rider can see the horse's eye. The outside rein acts as a restraint. Both hands gently follow the movement of the canter rhythm forwards, in order to enable the horse to stretch its neck.

The rider positions the horse in a slight bend to the inside with a low hand. Her middle position (region of the hips) flexibly follows the movement of the horse. Photo: Busch

The horse falls apart and only starts to canter after trotting faster and faster, like a carriage horse.

ADDITIONAL AIDS

VOICE

After the riding aids, the voice of the rider should be the most important aid of all. The rider can calm down a horse with his voice, encourage it and praise it. Most horses learn to accept the voice of their trainer right at the start of their training when they are lunged for the first time. The rider should praise his horse with his voice, if it has done something well, or calm it down, if it is frightened, shies or gets upset.

A practical voice aid is also the clicking of the tongue to encourage the horse to use its hindquarters more effectively and to place them further under its body, or to round its stride more at the canter. For this purpose, however, the horse will have to have learned to react to the rider's voice by increasing impulsion and tempo without leaning on the bit. The rider should practise this by clicking his tongue and at the same time restraining the horse, if it tries to rush off. If the horse then relaxes its lower jaw and does not push against the hand, the rider must praise it. This exercise should be stopped after two or three successful executions. It is important, however, that the rider only uses the voice as and when necessary and does not click his tongue continuously, as this would soon blunt the horse's reaction to the voice.

USE OF THE WHIP

The whip should never be used as an instrument of punishment, but should be used exclusively to encourage the impulsion of the horse, and when riding dressage for the purposeful employment of the individual legs of the horse. For jumping, the whip helps keep the forward propulsion of the horse going or to give the last necessary impulse at the moment of take-off. However, the rider should be warned not to make excessive use of the whip at any time, as it blunts the horse's reaction. The best way is to ride only a part of each lesson with the whip and place it on the side when not using it for specific exercises. Under no circumstances should the rider replace his aids by using the whip, but only apply it to support the natural aids. The sensitivity of the rider's legs cannot be replaced by the use of the whip.

USE OF THE SPURS

Spurs certainly have a practical use to ensure the fine-tuning of the horse's acceptance of the aids, as long as they are used with care. Constantly poking the horse's sides with the spurs only leads to a desensitisation of the horse to sharper and sharper spurs, if not even to open resistance on part of the horse. Young horses should be schooled from

Assistance not punishment! Spurs and whip fine-tune the application of the aids – if used correctly.

the start to observe the light aids of the rider's legs. If they do not react to them, the rider should intensify his aid for a short period of time by pressing the spur lightly against the horse's side. As soon as the horse shows the required reaction, the rider immediately returns to using the leg aid to drive the horse forward. For this purpose, it is necessary that the rider, on the one hand, has the position of his calves under control at all times (the spurs must not touch the horse's side except

when required), and on the other hand concentrates on whether and how the horse responds to his aids. Only then can the rider be sure that his horse will react sensitively to the leg aids permanently.

In the case of horses which have already been spoilt, the rider should also attempt to re-school the horse to accept light aids without spurs, by differing the intensity of the aids applied. In such cases, the corrective measures may require a long time.

THE RIDER´S FEEL

After having learned the technique of applying the rider's aids, the rider's feel is an essential aspect on the journey to becoming a good rider. It is not enough to apply the right aids; the rider also has to have the feeling when to correctly apply which aids with which intensity. In addition, he has to learn to combine the aids in such a way that he can make the horse understand harmoniously what he wants from it.

The rider has to learn when to apply his aids and in which combination in order to get the horse to relax and accept the bit. For this purpose, it is necessary to observe the reactions of the horse closely. It should feel well and work willingly with the rider. Because every horse is different and there is no general rule of how to ride every horse, the rider himself, or with the help of a riding instructor, will have to find out which is the best way to get his horse to co-operate.

During riding lessons, the rider should take note when he is instructed by the riding instructor to apply certain aids. If his horse has a tendency to fall apart and become long and flat, the rider will almost certainly have to frequently apply half-halts, in order to improve the posture of the horse.

If the horse has a tendency to rush off, it will certainly make sense to repeatedly ride it increasingly onto its hindquarters and to ride frequent transitions. The rider should think about where his problems lie and where the

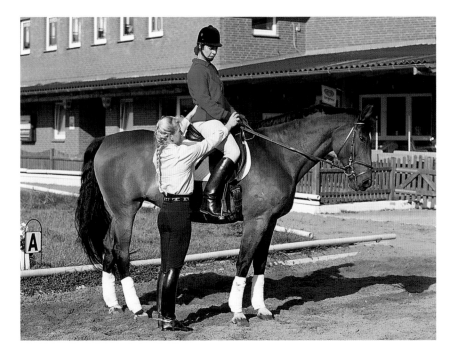

Each person learns differently. Corrections of the seat on the horse sharpen the rider's consciousness for the harmonious co-ordination of the rider's aids.

The commands of the riding instructor should be tailored to suit each individual pupil. Teaching in large groups is pointless.

problems of the horse lie and should concentrate specifically on these problems in each riding lesson.

As already mentioned, it is necessary to combine all aids correctly in order to achieve a good result. In this context, we would point out the tendency of most riders to do too much with the hands. Many riders ride with more intensive rein aids than back and leg aids. This is something every rider should try to counteract. Corrections in this area are usually forgotten after a passage of time and the rider will start to pull increasingly on the reins again. This is a matter for the rider to work on. He should continuously ask himself whether he could possibly ride with slightly lighter hands and should always try to give the reins. At the same time, he needs to ensure that he is activating the hindquarters sufficiently with his aids to create impulsion. Constant self-control on the part of the rider is required to achieve a steady success.

Riding is not just a form of sport, but primarily a partnership between human and horse. Therefore, one of the most important aims should be to develop the trust between the human and horse. Horses which feel that they are being treated correctly and whose riders show a capacity for intuitive power and understanding, will find work far more enjoyable, and this will be reflected in the horse's willingness to try its best and in positive training results.

Horses need praise just as much as humans do. They are pleased if they have fulfilled their task well and the rider rewards them for this. In this case they will be happy to repeat the task, remembering the positive experience. On the other hand, however, negative experiences also remain in the horse's memory. If they have not executed certain lessons correctly, because they had not been prepared sufficiently by the rider, for example, or because the rider did not apply his aids in a

Praise is important. It can come in many different forms. Words, patting of the neck, or immediate giving of the reins after a successfull movement. Whether or not the horse is proud of itself depends on the rider

way the horse could understand and the horse has been punished by the rider for its failure, this lesson will develop into a lesson of fear for the horse, which it will continue to connect with the negative experience well into the future. To correct this, the same exercise or a simpler version of it should be repeated quietly and patiently, until the horse has executed it better (not perfectly). Then the horse should be praised lavishly and the practice of this exercise stopped for the day. In this way, the horse does not have a negative experience to connect the task with and may well execute it a bit better, the next time it is asked to perform it.

One imperative characteristic of the rider has to be endless patience. Many riders assume that the horse is immediately able to perform all tasks expected of it, as long as the rider applies the correct aids. In reality the horse has to be prepared for each exercise and pace through continuous gymnastic exercises. It needs to develop the muscles required for the tasks and to be able to balance itself and the rider in an upright, collected posture. The horse will only let the rider teach it a new lesson step by step and without resistance, if it has been prepared sufficiently and is physically able to execute the exercise.

The rider needs to develop a feeling for the level to which he can ride his horse at any given moment, and when he is likely to be expecting too much of it. Impatient riders, in particular, tend to make excessive demands of their horse and thereby encourage it to resist the rider. The following general rule applies: the horse is not ready for anything that it is not willing to do without using force on part of the rider. It is not possible, for example, to do lateral work with a horse which has not learned to shift it weight onto it hindquarters sufficiently and is not balanced enough. Pulling the horse around by force will not lead to success in this case.

RIDING TRANSITIONS

One of the most important criteria for the schooling of the horse is the practice of transitions, as these improve the rhythm and balance of the horse and its responsiveness to the bit without resistance. Riding transitions also improve the willingness of the horse to collect itself, as well as the development of impulsion of the horse. For this reason, transitions should always form part of the daily work routine.

To begin with, the transitions from the walk to the halt are practised. Later the transition to the halt can also be practised from the trot and canter.

WALK TO HALT

One of the easiest transitions is the change of pace from the halt to the walk and from the walk to the halt. In the case of lazy horses, the first steps forward may be delayed. In this case, the sensitivity of the horse to the rider's legs should be improved by short forceful leg aids. The rider lightly rests the lower legs against the horse's sides and nudges the horse energetically once or makes use of the spurs, if the horse does not move off at the walk as soon as the light aids are applied. Afterwards, light aids are used again.

When bringing the horse to a halt, the rider needs to make sure that the horse is not pulled to a stop by the body and to stop the movement of the hips with his legs closed against the horse. As soon as the horse comes to a halt, the reins should be relaxed and the horse should be allowed to chew the reins out of the rider's hands and stretch its neck by lengthening the reins. As a rule, the rider should make the horse halt until it stands quietly and squarely on all four legs and flexes its poll.

Transitions should not look like this. The rider is standing in the stirrups and the horse is pressing down its spine to avoid the aids. The rider should not pull at the horse during the transition.

By using aids to increase impulsion, the rider encourages the horse to push its hindquarters under its centre of balance during the transition. Photo: Busch

The rider sits deep and well in the saddle and prepares the transition to the halt with half-halts. The hind-quarters are well forward under the horse's body.
Photo: Busch

If the horse frees itself during the motion to halt, the rider should only indicate the halt to practise the exercise and immediately drive the horse forwards again, while ensuring that the horse flexes its poll and uses its hindquarters. He will only allow the horse to stand still, if the latter does not push against the hand. After a few patient tries, the horse will remain on the bit willingly during a full halt, and the rider is able to praise it and terminate the exercise. In the case of horses which have an irregular beat at the walk, this exercise should only be ridden at the trot, in order not to endanger the rhythm at the walking pace.

In order to correct the horse's acceptance of the bit and contact with the rider's hand after a full halt, the rider can restrain the hand aid immediately after the horse, which is fighting the rein, comes to a halt, until the horse drops its head and flexes the poll. However, the rider must not pull at the reins but only

hold them steady instead of giving. It is important to use the driv-ing aids to create impulsion at the same time. Should the horse raise its head even higher, the rider should shorten the reins a little bit further; if the horse stretches its neck down, the reins are lengthened in proportion to the downward extension of the neck until it willingly drops its neck. Then the reins are released bilaterally and the horse is praised. This way the horse learns that accepting the bit and maintaining soft contact with the rider's hand is always more comfortable if it lowers its poll until it has reached the correct posture, and that any upward stretching of the neck is always going to become more and more unpleasant.

The rider should, however, as a rule ensure that the horse does not hold its head too low at the halt and tenses the neck shortening the forehand. The neck should be stretched forwards in a relaxed position and the horse's mouth

The horse comes to a correct closed halt standing square and with its hindquarters well underneath its body. Photo: Busch

should not lie below the point of the shoulder. Often the horse resists acceptance of the bit and avoids the contact with the rider's hand at the halt because it is forced into an unpleasant foreshortened posture. The rider must avoid this at all costs. On the contrary, the halt should be made as pleasant as possible for the horse, because it will then stop willingly and with pleasure.

Standing Square and Closed

The closed and square halt is achieved, if the horse places its hindquarters well under its body at the moment of the full halt rein aid and simultaneous aids of the rider to create impulsion. To begin with, the whip can be used to correct the position of the individual legs after the horse has come to a standstill, in order to make the horse understand what the rider requires it to do. If the closed position, however, is subsequently only achieved with the aid of the whip, the schooling has gone

wrong, as this only makes the horse nervous and it will have difficulties in standing still calmly. Also this will only lead to a mechanical closing of the legs, not to a placing of the hindquarters under the horse's body and distribution of weight to the hind legs.

In order to bring the hind legs of the horse under its centre of balance, the rider will have to collect the horse increasingly before using the full halt to come to a standstill and encourage the horse to bring its hindquarters forwards more.

It is recommended that the tempo should be shortened shortly before coming to a halt to the point of collection in order to prevent the horse from braking on its forehand. During the halt the rider encourages the horse to carry its head up in position with restraining rein aids. The horse is able to place its hindquarters further under its body and halt more squarely, if it is allowed to carry its head high with a flexed poll and in gentle contact with the rider's hand.

During the halt, the rider needs to encourage the horse to take a step further with its hind legs by using leg and seat aids, driving the horse forward. This ensures that the hind legs are placed underneath the horse's body and the horse will automatically place its legs squarely in a closed position in order to retain its balance. The rider's hips need to give the forward-moving hindquarters the necessary space. This means that the rider will feel how first one and then the other hind leg is placed under the horse's centre of balance, thus pushing the hip slightly forward.

In order to practise this, the rider will allow the horse to step forwards again with its hind legs at the halt. The rider will only support the driving aid with the whip or spurs for a moment, if the horse does not accept the leg aids during this exercise.

At the same time, the reins will absorb the motion softly, if the horse places its weight on the reins. Pulling down the horse's head during the halt is a common fault. During the halt, the horse should retain its upright posture, so that the forward and upward motion is maintained during the full halt.

In order to practise this, it is possible just to indicate the intention of halting and then stimulate the hindquarters to keep on moving forwards. This exercise will lead to one or two steps on the spot, followed by immediate moving forward at the previous pace.

The correction of the position of the legs with the whip should be carried out by an assistant on the ground. He will tap the hind leg which is further back. The horse is praised immediate-

ly, if it reacts. It is not important in this context that the horse places the corrected hind leg parallel to the other hind leg, but only that it moves it forwards. The corrective measure with the whip should only be carried out once, in order not to disconcert the horse. The horse will learn to close the legs correctly with an improved feeling of balance. The horse would not understand excessive correction and the effect would be a negative one.

TROT TO WALK

The transitions between the trot and the walk are very easy in comparison. In order to encourage the horse to trot, it is important to prepare the horse sensitively for the driving aids to create impulsion. When changing down a pace to the walk, it should suffice if the rider stretches his upper body and restrains the movement of the horse with the hips and thighs while keeping the hands steady. The rider needs to make sure that he does not use the restraining aids for too long and cause the horse to come to a complete halt. As soon as the transition begins, the rider will start riding a free and even medium walk using the driving aids. The transitions should flow as smoothly as possible and without any interruption of the impulsion.

TROT TO HALT

Moving away at a trot from the halt requires a sensitive reaction on the part of the horse to the driving leg aids. In addition, the horse should not fall apart during the halt but should retain its impulsion in response to the leg aids. During the halt, the rider will keep his legs closed in order to be able to ride the horse forward at any given time. Any backward movement of the horse is counted as a fault. When changing down from the trot to the halt, the same aids are applied as for the transition from the walk to the halt. The important thing here is the increased collection of the horse at the trot before the transition. The rider needs to take care that he does not fall forwards with his upper body at the halt or that his legs slip forwards. These should remain closed evenly around the horse's sides.

CANTER TO TROT

Cantering from the trot is achieved through a supple aid to canter from the flexible hip swinging with the motion of the horse, and the legs. The impulse for the horse to launch into a canter comes from the inner hip, which is pushed forward, and the inner leg on the girth. During the transition from the canter to the trot it is important not to lose rhythm or cause an irregularity of the gait. The horse should make the transition from the canter to the trot smoothly and as directly as possible without losing tempo. Before the transition, the horse is collected slightly at the canter. For the introduction of the transition, the rider no longer moves his inner hip forward at the canter, but instead pushes both hips forward at the trot rhythm. The reins are restrained only for a short period. The legs remain closed at the horse's sides

for a moment. As soon as the horse takes its first steps at the trot, the rider drives the horse forwards at the new rhythm without interruption.

CANTER TO WALK

Usually, cantering from the walk does not present any particular problems. It simply requires a sensitive reaction of the horse to the aids. In order to practise this exercise, transitions from the walk to the canter are ridden on a circle. Here, the aids should initially be given as lightly as possible, and only if the horse does not immediately start cantering with impulsion, should the rider intensify the aids for a short moment. In addition, the voice (clicking of the tongue) can also be used to help gain the horse's attention. Cantering from the walk is particularly suitable to improve the canter of the horse and to prepare it for collection.

The transition from the canter to the walk is slightly more difficult. The danger is that the horse may fall too heavily onto the forehand during the transition, if it is not balanced enough yet with its weight on the hindquarters. The prerequisite for this transition is the shortened or collected canter. Only when the horse has learned to carry its weight on its hindquarters at the canter can it be slowed down to a walk without falling apart. The rider prepares the horse for the transition through a number of half-halts and imagines that he is riding the canter on one spot. This ensures that he keeps the horse in a well-set upright posture. Then he leaves the legs closed, stops moving the inner hip forwards and

In order to prepare the horse for the transition to the walk, the rider collects the pace at the canter and makes sure that the poll remains the highest point of the horse. The inner leg should drive the horse forwards better on the girth.
Photograph: Busch

of the rider's body will maintain the impulsion of the movement of the horse, so it immediately walks forwards at the walk. The transition should be smooth and certainly not halting. Afterwards, the rider must ensure, with his aids driving the horse forward in the rhythm of the pace, that the horse will stride forward at a relaxed medium walk. As the rhythm at the walk is often bound directly after the canter, there is a danger that the horse will move with a rack-like rhythm. Never start the next exercise or a renewed canter until the horse is walking at a clear rhythmic walk.

In the beginning, the rider should allow a slower transition with a few steps at the trot instead of using the reins too much, as this would encourage the horse to resist the aids, and will later cause it to push against the hand during all transitions. It is better to keep the hands soft and to praise the horse for a successful performance and then terminate the exercise. It will learn the exercise much faster this way. In the advanced stage, the transitions can simply be indicated for practice purposes. The rider restrains the driving aids for a moment so that the horse starts to prepare to halt. At that moment the rider will reapply the driving aids to continue to canter. This improves the horse's responsiveness and relaxation, and the rider can improve the horse's acceptance of the bit and contact with the rider's hand during the change of pace.

It should be said generally that the transitions need to be practised all the time in order to maintain the horse's suppleness and flexibility.

keeps the fists with the reins steady. Initially it is better if the rider also uses his voice to make the horse understand what he wants, instead of pulling on the reins, thus causing the horse to resist the exercise. During the transition the rider needs to make sure that he does not pull in the horse's neck and head, as this will make it impossible for the horse to balance itself and it will thus transfer its weight on the reins. Although the inside leg and hip no longer drive the horse forwards, the slight tensioning

DRESSAGE MOVEMENT AND EXERCISES

RIDING INTO CORNERS

During daily schooling work, the rider should always practise correct riding of corners, as this improves the horse's bend and straightness.

Approximately three metres before the corner the rider asks for the horse to bend inward. The inside leg acts on the girth to assist the horse to bend its spine correctly to the inside. The outside lower leg is placed a hand's width behind the girth as a restraining aid to stop the horse's hindquarters from swinging out. Now the inside leg drives the horse deep into the corner. At the same time, the bend of the horse's ribcage must increase. Often the forehand of the horse moves far into the corner, which is incorrect, however, and will lead to the hindquarters falling inwards. That way, the horse does not need to bend. Therefore, the most important factor is the bending influence of the inside leg and the position of the neck determined by the inside hand. At the innermost point of the corner both reins are relaxed slightly in order to allow the horse actively to step under with its hindlegs.

Before riding into a corner the horse is bent to the inside. The outside leg stops the hindquarters from swinging outward, while the inside leg has the main task of maintaining impulsion, and acts resting at the girth. Photo: Busch

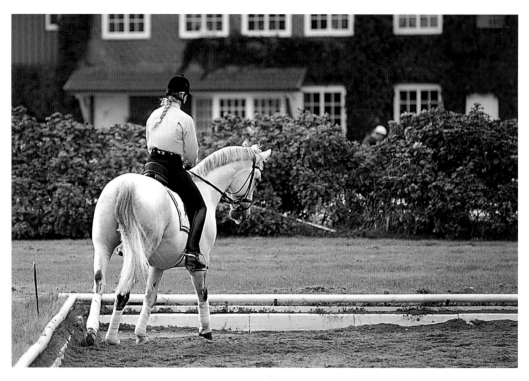

The outside rein should not remain fixed and immobile in one position, but should give the same amount as the inside hand is asking for the bend.

CHANGING THE REIN DIAGONALLY ACROSS THE SCHOOL

Riding into corners correctly is the prerequisite of turning correctly at the turning point of the school to change diagonally across the whole school or half of the school. When the horse's shoulder is parallel with the turning point, the rider turns the horse, which is already bent to the inside (from coming out of the corner) away from the track with the outside leg and slight pressure of the outside rein. As soon as the horse has been turned away from the track it is straightened out so it strides out evenly, seeking contact with both reins. The rider will keep the horse straight until they reach the diagonally opposite turning point. The horse is not bent to the other side until it has actually reached the turning

point. Changing the horse over from one leg to the other too early may mean that the hindquarters swing out, thus leading to the horse arriving at the turning point too early, and crooked. The horse should reach the turning point when its shoulders are parallel with it.

RIDING A 20-METRE CIRCLE

During this movement, the rider needs to make sure that the circle is perfectly round and that the horse is bent continuously lengthwise. The inside leg drives the horse forward on the girth in rhythm with the movement, the outside leg acts as a restraint behind the girth. During the entire circle, the horse remains uniformly positioned and bent from poll to tail. This will provide the correct circle, without the need for the reins to give any addition-

On the diagonal track, the horse should move from turning point to turning point perfectly straight. The leg aids are applied evenly and maintain rhythm and impulsion. The horse only changes over to the other rein, once it has reached the turning point.

al directions. On the open side of the circle, the outside leg is applied more actively to act as a replacement for the ring fence and to keep the horse's hindquarters in line. On the closed side of the circle, the inside leg increas-

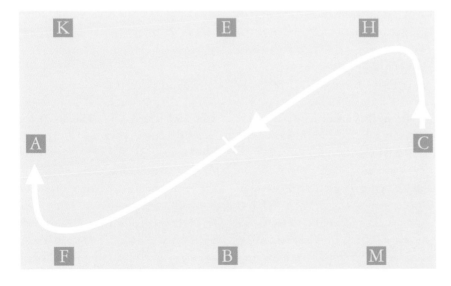

Changing the rein diagonally across the school

The horse is bent evenly along the longitudinal axis while straight in itself. The hind legs step precisely into the tracks of the forelegs. The inside leg maintains the bend, the outside leg controls the hindquarters.

ingly provides the bend. As a rule, when riding circles and turns, the rider needs to observe that the horse is straight in itself on its vertical axis. The hind feet need to step into the prints of the front feet.

inside leg and seat bone. He should avoid pulling around the horse's head by the reins. The change from one rein to the other should be carried out as smoothly and harmoniously as possible.

CHANGING THE REIN IN A FIGURE OF EIGHT FROM A CIRCLE

Shortly before reaching the centre of the school (X), the rider straightens out his horse and rides it forwards for one horse's length, preparing the bend to the other side with his new

CHANGING THE REIN THROUGH THE CIRCLE

At the centre point of the circle before the open side the rider turns the horse into a 10-metre half-volte. In the centre of the circle. he changes his horse's bend from one rein to the other and rides another 10-metre half-volte to

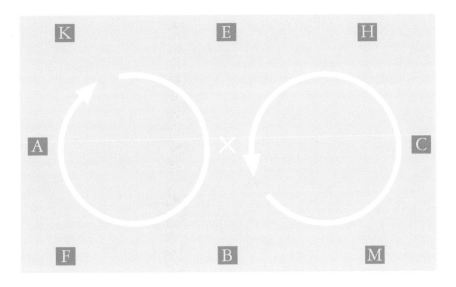

Riding a 20-metre circle

the opposite point of the circle. The most important thing to pay attention to in this movement is the correct riding of the two 10-metre half-voltes. The change of rein and bend should be introduced by the respective new inside leg. By hollowing itself laterally to the new inner side, the horse will perform the turn willingly without any necessity for the rider to pull the horse around by the reins. Changing the reins through the 20-metre circle and the following difficult turns should be practised at the walk to begin with, and later at the working trot.

SIMPLE SERPENTINE

The simple serpentine is ridden on the long side of the school from one turning point to the other with a distance

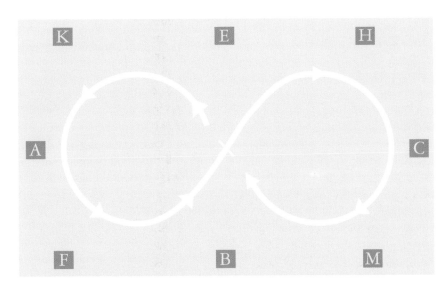

Changing reins in a figure of eight from a circle

of 5 metres to the track at the widest point of the loop. The horse is already bent to the inside coming out of the corner and is turned off the track at the turning point. As soon as the horse has been turned off the track, the new inside leg (the outside leg up to now) is applied on the girth in order to turn the horse into the new bend and to encourage it to hollow itself laterally on its new inner side. The rein ensures that the neck position is changed, but is otherwise not involved in the change of direction. The entire loop is now ridden with the horse bent uniformly from poll to tail.

Shortly before reaching the second turning point, the horse is again bent around the other way with the original inside leg applied on the girth. The outside aids in turn ensure that the horse does not fall apart in the bend and that the hind legs follow the tracks of the front legs precisely. If the rider sits correctly, the changed position of the rider's legs in the bend will automatically ensure that the inside seat bone bears the greater weight.

DOUBLE SERPENTINE

The aids for the double serpentine are the same as those for the single serpentine. In this movement, however, two flatter loops (maximum distance from the track 2.5 metres) are required and the tempo is slower reaching the point of collection. The immediate repeated change of direction means that the horse needs to be particularly supple and responsive to the aids. If horse and rider experience difficulties in this movement, particular attention should be paid to the changeovers. The serpentine is created by the repeated immediate lateral hollowing out of the horse to the right and the left.

As soon as one side of the horse is hollow (bent inward), the rider has to transfer his weight to the other side and change the position of his legs in order to encourage the horse to hol-

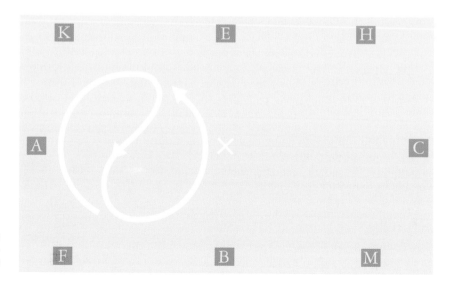

Changing the rein through the 20-metre circle

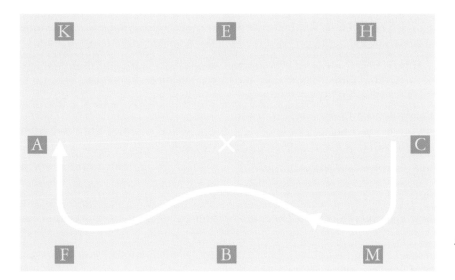

Simple serpentine

low out its ribcage in the other direction. One grave error here, in particular, is excessive use of the reins. This will only bend the horse in line with the serpentine with its head and neck; the body and the hindquarters, however, swing outward instead. At the same time, the rider needs to ensure that the horse actively places its hind legs under the body and distributes its weight on its hindquar-

ters, so that it does not lose impulsion and fall apart. In order to practise this movement, a series of larger loops can be ridden in a larger area (for example a field) without the restriction of the ring fence. Here, the rider should simply make sure that the loops are introduced solely through the influence of the rider's legs.

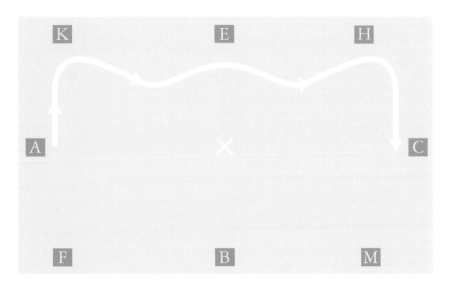

Double serpentine

SERPENTINE WITH LOOPS TOUCHING THE SIDE OF THE ARENA

Depending on the number of loops, these are distributed evenly over the length of the school. The first turn away from the track, as well as the last turn back on it, already count as loops. In a serpentine with three loops on a 20 x 40-metre school the first loop begins around two to three metres after the first point of the circle. The highest point of the second loop is exactly at the middle of the opposite long side of the school (B or E). In the case of four loops, one loop is executed before the point of the circle and one loop behind it. The line across the half of the school (B to E) separates the second and the third loop. Each turn-off from the track is executed in the form of a half-volte. After the half-volte, the horse is straightened and hollowed out and changed over to the other side while being ridden over the centre line (A to C). The difficulty in this movement is changing over the horse on the straight lines between the half-voltes, without the horse swinging out its hindquarters or wavering from the straight line. This is only possible if the horse is fixed in position with reins and permits the rider to bend it and hollow out its ribcage in the new direction with the legs. Steering the horse with the reins is incorrect and will always lead to wavering and evasive hindquarters. The forward-driving aids ensure that the horse steps out with impulsion with its hind legs during the entire serpentine.

TURN ON THE FOREHAND

The turn on the forehand is especially suited to teaching the horse the lateral aids. During the turn on the forehand, the hind legs of the horse turn around the turning point which is situated close to the inside foreleg. For the half-turn, the horse is turned around by 90 degrees, at the full turn to the right or left, the turn is 180 degrees.

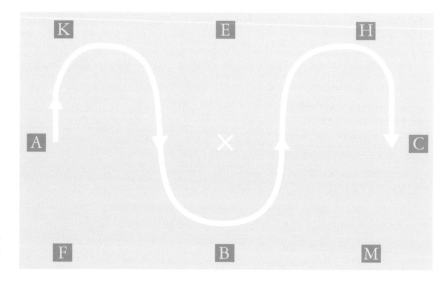

Serpentine of three loops touching the sides of the arena.

In order to introduce the movement, the rider should stop the horse on the second track about 1.5 metres from the fence; otherwise, the horse will knock its head against the fence during the turn. Once the horse has come to a collected halt on the bit, the rider bends it in the opposite direction of the intended movement, i.e. if it is on the left rein, bend the horse to the right, and vice versa. The outside rein acts as a restraint and prevents the horse from being bent too far to the inside. The inside leg (in this case the right leg) is applied a hand's width behind the girth and drives the horse sideways. The outside leg, also a hand's width behind the girth, acts as a restraint. It receives and regulates the movement of the horse at every second step and prevents the horse from swinging around too quickly and the hindquarters from falling apart. The laterally pushing rider's leg encourages the horse to cross over sideways with its inside leg in front of the outside leg. If the horse does not react immediately to the aids, some riders attempt the start of the lateral movement by bending the horse further.

This is a serious fault because it does not teach the horse to pay more attention to the lateral driving leg, which is the whole reason for this exercise. Therefore, the rider should never induce the turn around the forehand with the reins but instead, should give an active impulse with his inside leg and if necessary nudge the horse with his calf or use the whip or spur. Immediately afterwards lighten, the aids again. If the horse moves sideways, the

During the turn of the forehand, the horse turns around the inside foreleg (here, the right foreleg) with its hind legs. The forelegs of the horse move on the spot. Here, the rider is leaning over too far to the right and bends in the right hip, moving the seat bones to the left. This means that the left leg cannot rest against the horse's side.

lateral movement should be received and regulated with the outer leg after every second step, before the inside leg restarts the lateral leg aid, until the horse has completed a turn of 180 degrees. For practising purposes, a horse which tends to rush around can be restrained after each step and encouraged to chew on the bit, relaxing its lower jaw. The rider ensures that the horse accepts and maintains contact with the bit during the entire turn, with the correct rein aids.

The position must be maintained. At the same time the rider prevents the horse from stepping forwards with the reins, and taking a step backwards by relaxing the pressure on the reins and using the seat and legs to drive the horse forwards. If performed correctly, the turn around the forehand is a very useful exercise to fine-tune the effect of the leg aids, and should be practised frequently.

LEG-YIELDING

In the same way as the turn on the forehand, leg-yielding also improves the responsiveness and ability of the horse to accept the bit and the aids, as well as the lateral aids. It thereby, on the one hand, enables the rider to have a greater influence on his horse and, on the other hand, improves the sensitivity of the horse to the lateral aids of the rider. Leg-yielding along the length of the school is a forwards-sideways movement during which the horse moves along the track at an angle of no more than 45 degrees. To begin with, it is easier to let the horse yield to the outside leg: in other words turn the horse with its head towards the ring fence. At a more advanced level, leg-yielding is performed primarily with the head towards the centre of the school, as this teaches the horse to accept the rein aids more. The horse is driven sideways at the walking pace with the inside laterally driving leg, which is applied a hand's width behind the girth. The outer leg also rests against the horse one hand's width behind the girth, but has a restraining effect, i.e., it prevents the horse from turning more than 45 degrees from the track on the one hand. On the other it is used actively (on the girth), if the horse loses the forward impulsion and no longer steps forwards-sideways sufficiently enough. The weight of the rider is distributed unilaterally on the inside seat bone, dictated automatically by the position of the rider's legs. The rein aids position the horse slightly to the side of the laterally applied leg. The outside rein prevents the horse from moving too far sideways, a position often incorrectly used to introduce and maintain the lateral movement. This, however, does not help the horse improve its reaction to the lateral leg aids. After riding the horse correctly into the corner, the rider turns his horse towards the centre of the school or facing the fence. He needs to ensure that the horse is not bent further than the second or third cervical vertebra.

Initially, the leg aids are applied lightly in time with the hind leg that the horse is lifting up. However if the horse does not react the rider should use greater force in applying the aids. A rider's lower leg, pushed constantly against the horse's side will not trigger the desired lateral movement. The rider gives the horse short impulses in time with the hind leg lifting up. The intensity of the aids is dependent on the performance of the horse. If the horse fails to react, the whip or spur are applied for a short time, to increase the sensitivity of the horse. Afterwards, the rider reverts to especially light aids. In the case of horses which hurry sideways or forwards, it can help to bring the horse to a halt during the leg-yielding movement. In this instance, the horse remains bent as it was for the lateral movement. It should be encouraged to chew on the bit and relax its lower jaw. Then the inside leg can increase the bend of the horse's hindquarters, if necessary, before commencing with the lateral movement. Under no circumstances should the horse be positioned vertically to the track, as this would cause it to lose all necessary forward impulsion.

LEG-YIELDING TOWARDS THE CENTRE OF THE SCHOOL AND BACK OUT

For this movement, the horse is ridden forwards-sideways parallel to the long side of the school. It should step over forwards evenly across the outside legs and the forehand should always lead. This lesson is very instructive as the rider learns to influence the horse in

Leg-yielding on the diagonal. The horse is bent against the direction of the movement in the second and third cervical vertebrae. The outside rein (seen from the front) prevents the horse from bending too far. The outside leg should lie more firmly against the horse's side.

the direction of the movement. Leg-yielding towards the centre of the school starts at the first turning point of the long side of the school. As a preparation, the rider drives the horse's hindquarters deep into the corner and then bends the horse slightly to the outside. The rider should avoid bending the horse too far. Then he places the leg on the side of the fence behind the girth and using the lateral leg aid drives the horse sideways. The rider's

new outside leg is placed behind the girth to receive and regulate the impulsion and to prevent the hindquarters from swinging outward. The outside leg can also become active on the girth to drive the horse forwards, if it does not move forwards (sideways) with enough impulsion.

The outside rein leads the horse towards the centre of the school and ensures that the forehand leads the movement (it should lead by at least

The inside leg (left leg of the rider) drives the horse sideways behind the girth when the horse's inside hind leg lifts up. The outside leg regulates the lateral movement behind the girth and, if necessary, drives the horse forward on the girth. Photo: Busch

one step ahead). The inside rein ensures that the horse maintains its bend flexibly. The rider's weight is automatically shifted to the inside seat bone through the position of the rider's legs. Once the horse has reached a point equidistant between the outside track and the centre line (five metres away from the track and the centre line), the horse is ridden straight ahead for three strides. Here, it is important that the horse walks forwards freely

and in rhythm. Then it is bent to the other side and ridden forwards-sideways laterally inverted to the second turning point of the long side of the school.

For practising purposes, it makes sense initially to practise the two parts of the movement separately. For this purpose, the rider should change the rein diagonally through the school, asking the horse to leg-yield all the way. It gives the horse more time to adjust itself to the lateral movement. In order to practise the straight walk in the middle section, the rider can repeatedly ride forwards a few steps during the change of rein across the school. He should ensure that the horse walks with a clear four-beat and walks forwards without hesitation.

LEG-YIELDING AT THE TROT

Once the horse has learned to perform leg-yielding at the walk well, the movement can also be ridden at a slow, well-collected trot. This is a preparation for the more advanced lateral work

(where the horse is bent in the direction of the movement) and it improves the influence the rider has on the horse. To begin with, the rider rides the horse forwards-sideways three to four metres away from the track, using the same aids as for leg-yielding towards the centre of the school and back out, and then after a few straight strides pushes the horse laterally back towards the track. This improves the sensitivity of the horse towards the leg aids enormously. The horse learns not to stick to the track and to react promptly and sensitively to the laterally acting back and leg aids of the rider.

When performing leg-yielding at the trot, the rider has to make sure

If the horse has learned to perform leg-yielding at the walk well, the exercise can be practised at the slow trot. With a relaxed horse which responds to the rider's aids and a balanced rider, the step towards advanced lateral work is now only a short one.

that the trot does not become too free and that the horse is bent only slightly, so that it does not knock its legs by overreaching. The rider uses the same aids as during the walk, but has to observe in particular that his hips swing flexibly with the motion of the horse and supports it actively.

The rider encourages the horse to use its hindlegs with impulsion during the lateral movement, by using the driving back and leg aids. The reins need to be held more flexibly than at the walk in order not to disrupt the horse's forward impulsion. The horse should have learned at the walk to accept the laterally driving rider's leg without storming off forwards and leaning on the rein. Once the horse has learned to leg-yield away from the long side of the school, the rider can start practising leg-yielding along the long side of the school, either yielding the outside leg (with the head turned to the fence) or the inside leg (with the head turned towards the centre of the school). Short stretches are better than long ones.

VOLTES

When riding a volte, the horse is expected to bend laterally as far as it is capable of, depending on the diameter of the circle. The size of the volte, therefore, needs to be adapted to the training stage of the horse. Pulling the horse around into as tight a volte as possible simply leads to resistance on the part of the horse, while in no way improving the bend. The best way to start is by making the normal circle smaller until the horse performs a volte at the centre of the circle. During this movement, the horse's neck should be as stretched out as far as possible so that the horse is able to maintain its balance. The rider's inside leg supplies the bend and prevents the hindquarters from falling inward in a traverse movement. The outside leg restrains the hindquarters and, if necessary, makes the volte smaller. The rider's weight is centered on the inside seat bone. The inside rein leads the horse into the turn and maintains the position. It needs to be held lightly during the volte and must under no circumstances pull the horse, as this could easily lead to a lateral over-bending of the neck. The outside rein acts as a restraint and can lead to the straightness of the horse, if pressed lightly against the neck. In order to regulate the tempo, the rider will ride half-halts as and when necessary. Once the horse has learned to perform voltes within the circle well, the rider should ride voltes from the track towards the centre of the school. He must ensure that the voltes are round. It is important to flex and bend the horse inwards one horse's length before reaching the point at which the horse leaves the track. The outside rein and inside leg make sure that the horse does not leave the track too early. In this connection, the inside leg should not be applied rigidly, as this causes discomfort to the horse. A flexible leg moving with the motion of the horse is a far more pleasant experience for the horse. As soon as the horse's shoulder has reached the turning point, the outside rider's leg is applied actively and the reins give slightly to let the horse move forward into the turn. Now the volte has to be ridden as an even circle

The inside rein regulates the bend for the introduction of the volte. The outside rein is lengthened accordingly and then acts as a restraint. Here, the rider should make sure that the horse does not drop its nose too low. Photograph: Busch

from the start. The outside leg prevents the hindquarters from swinging out, which would make the volte take the shape of an ellipse.

The rider's hips should remain as relaxed as possible and swing forwards with the motion of the horse in order to maintain impulsion and support the movement. For practising purposes the voltes can be ridden in the corners of the school. This also improves riding into corners.

REIN-BACK

If carried out correctly the rein-back is a valuable lesson as it improves the horse's acceptance of the bit and responsiveness as well as its balance and suppleness.

By bending its hindlegs at a more acute angle, the horse's ability to go at collected paces is supported at the same time. In the wild, moving backwards means that in a fight regarding the order of rank within the herd, the horse is giving in to its stronger opponent. Therefore, using the rein-back in equitation also means a submission of the horse towards its rider. For this reason, some horses regard it as a punishment. Therefore, the rider should not ask the horse to rein back too often and should terminate the exercise, if it has been executed correctly.

At the rein-back the horse strides backwards in "two-time" as in the trot. Therefore, we talk of strides, not steps. The sequence of strides is only clear, and the horse will only pick up its feet while willingly going on the bit, instead of dragging the feet through the sand, if it is responsive and strides backwards with a relaxed back. To begin with the horse is asked to rein

The rider's legs (inside leg on the girth - outside leg one hand's width behind the girth) maintain the lateral bend of the horse. The position of the neck must never be more acute than the bend as the horse would then swing outward with its hindquarters. Photo: Busch

If the volte is ridden with a correct bend, the horse's forefeet and hind feet are placed down on the same circle line. The rider can check this on a smoothly raked sand-covered school . Photo: Busch

To initiate the rein-back, the aids are given asking the horse to move forwards, but using restraining rein aids at the same time. This causes the horse to transfer its impulsion to go forwards to reining back instead. If the horse is relaxed and on the bit it will step back in "two-time" with each diagonal pair of legs. Photograph: Busch

back one horse's length, i.e., three to four strides. Afterwards, the horse is either encouraged to walk forwards again at the walk with the appropriate driving aids, or asked to halt. If the horse is expected to halt, the last stride is in fact only half a stride (which however is counted as a full stride), in order to bring the horse to a halt in a square, closed position. In order to initiate the rein-back, it is essential that the horse is standing balanced on all four legs and relaxed in the poll and on the bit. If it is made to stand too long, the forward impulsion will be lost and it

becomes very difficult to initiate the rein-back. Therefore, the rider should always start the rein-back after a short calm halt. If the horse does not stand relaxed immediately after it has been asked to halt, the rider should practise asking the horse to come down on the bit and stretch forwards and downwards at the halt first. Trying to execute the rein-back at a too early stage would only cause damage, and the horse will start resisting the rider in this case.

A horse which reins back even before the rider has given the aids,

Both rider's legs are placed behind the girth to prevent the horse from swinging out to one side. Here, the horse does not stride back with supple relaxation. It is lying on the bit and not rounding its back correctly.

also needs to be corrected at the halt first. In this case, the rider will not perform the rein-back in the daily work routine, until the horse has learned to stand still while maintaining the forward impulsion. In order to ask the horse to rein back, the rider will give the same aids as those for moving forwards from a halt. As soon as he feels the forward impulsion of the horse, he transfers this backwards by not giving the reins (in fact, to begin with, by shortening the reins slightly). During the rein-back the rider relieves the pressure of the seat bones on the saddle by relaxing his back. Initially, the rider can lean his upper body forwards slightly in order to relieve the horse's back. At a more advanced stage, the relief of the pressure of the seat bones should be performed with the rider sitting upright. The rider hereby transfers his weight onto the upper part of the thighs. During the rein-back, the rider's legs rest against the horse's side in a restraining manner, to prevent the horse from swinging out sideways. Light leg aids in rhythm with the strides trigger a new stride backwards until the required number has been performed.

After transferring the forward impulsion backward, the reins are relaxed slightly, but without the rider losing contact with the horse's mouth. If necessary, the rider closes his hands lightly at every stride but always relaxes the reins after each stride. At the same time, the rein ensures that the horse remains correctly on the bit, by giving and taking right-left slightly, without, however, influencing the flow of movement.

During the rein-back, the horse must remain on the bit the whole time, as it will otherwise cease to round its back correctly. This makes the exercise unpleasant for the horse and will prevent it from repeating it willingly. If necessary, the horse should be corrected by asking for only one stride after halting squarely and relaxed with the horse on the bit. Then the horse has to be brought back on the bit before it is asked to take another stride back. At the same time, the rider needs to ensure that the horse does not become too tight in the neck, as this will prevent it from staying in balance and will also lead to resistance. Often the horse swings into the middle of the school with its hindquarters in order to avoid having to take the increased load on its hindquarters. In this case, the rider should bend the horse very slightly to the inside and keep the hindquarters out very decisively with the inside leg.

When teaching a young horse, it is very helpful to use the voice as an extra aid. The command "back", which the horse should have learned before it was even broken in, initially accompanies the rein-back. In the event of difficul-

ties, an assistant on the ground can push the horse backwards by using pressure on its chest. The horse will thus learn the rein-back much faster than if it is pulled back by the reins. It should be possible to terminate the rein-back and initiate the motion forwards at any time by using the appropriate aids. Any uncontrolled reining-back of the horse should be prevented at all costs as this gives the horse the opportunity to evade the rider's aids completely. This can culminate in the horse rearing up.

Therefore, to begin with, the horse will only be asked to move back one or two strides before it is encouraged to move forwards at the walk again immediately with the forwards driving aids. The rider should initiate each stride backwards anew and should pause slightly between the individual strides in the beginning. At an advanced stage, the horse can be asked to move forwards at the trot or even the canter, straight from the rein-back.

In order to ride the horse to a correct halt, square and closed in the end, the rider must maintain the forward impulsion. The forward driving aids are applied consistently in such a manner that the horse can be ridden forwards at any time. By stretching his upper body and pressing the lower legs against the horse's sides, the rider terminates the rein-back. He needs to initiate these aids after the second-last stride to ensure that the last stride becomes only a half-stride so that the horse comes to a square halt. If the position needs correction, the horse's hindlegs can be encouraged to move forwards into a close position with the correct aids.

VOLTES AT THE CANTER

Turns at the canter are always more difficult to perform than turns at the trot, as the horse finds it more difficult to keep its balance at the canter. Voltes at the canter, therefore, need to be prepared with particular care. A basic prerequisite to be able to ride a volte at the canter, is that the horse has learned to transfer its weight onto its hindlegs and canter collectedly. If the horse is collected and bent correctly, it should willingly canter an eight-metre volte. The engagement of the hindquarters and raised, almost vertical, position of the neck and head are maintained throughout. In order to practise this movement, the rider can start the canter on a circle and slowly decrease its size. The rider needs to make sure that the hindquarters remain engaged and that the horse is straight in itself on the vertical axis. The outside aids ensure that the horse's hindquarters do not fall out. In order to ensure an active engagement of the hindquarters, the rider can use his voice or a short tap with the whip to maintain impulsion.

Initially, the circle should not be decreased in size too much, nor should the horse be ridden at such a sharp bend for too long. The rider should only decrease the size of the circle to the extent to which he can bend the horse with his back and legs. Pulling the horse around with the reins should be avoided at all costs. Many riders have a tendency to tighten the horse's neck position at the volte. This means, however, that the horse cannot balance itself sufficiently and will resist the rider. The rider always needs to ensure that the horse's neck is stretched forwards (without losing contact with the horse's mouth). At the next stage, the rider practises turning the horse away from the track with the outside aids. Again, the voltes should be larger to begin with until the horse can balance its weight correctly and the rider can slowly begin to make the volte smaller. An excellent exercise to practise this is riding voltes at the trot in every corner and at the middle of the long sides of the school. If this exercise is performed daily for one or two circuits of the school, the bend as well as the active engagement of the hindquarters during the voltes, the horse will improve rapidly. Soon the voltes can be decreased to a diameter of eight metres. A positive side-effect is the improvement of the straightness of the horse in its vertical axis and the quality of the canter. The horse will also find riding into corners much easier to perform.

HALF-VOLTES AT THE CANTER BACK TO THE TRACK TO CHANGE REINS

Half-voltes at the canter back to the track to change reins can be ridden out of the second corner on the long side, or no later than at the middle of the long side. The first part of the half-volte is ridden like the normal volte at the canter. After half of the volte has been ridden, the rider terminates the volte and returns to the track, thereby changing the rein.

The horse should only be returned back to the track after five or six metres; this movement may not be carried out in the form of a half-pass. The rider initiates the volte as described above. At the point furthest from the track the rider straightens out the horse and rides it back to the trot in a straight line. Particular care should be taken to ride the horse forward with increased impulsion, ensuring that the outside aids are applied distinctly. A problem which often occurs when returning to the track is an exaggerated bend to the inside. This causes the horse's hindquarters to swing out and the horse becomes crooked. In this position it is impossible to continue to ride the horse forward correctly at the counter-canter. The rider should increase the application of the outside aids and only ask for a slight bend.

For practising purposes, the horse should initially perform voltes at the canter in the corners of the school. Once these are wellridden at the required radius, the rider can develop the half-volte from this movement.

COUNTER-CANTER

At the counter-canter the horse is asked to lead with the outside foreleg, contrary to the normal position. The outside of the school thus becomes the inside rein. The counter-canter is always ridden at the collected canter, to ensure that the horse can keep its balance sufficiently. Prerequisites for the

When riding the half-volte at the canter back to the track to change the rein, the restraining outside aids need to be applied with particular care. Here the horse is bent correctly. However, the rider should shorten her reins before riding the half-volte.
Photo: Busch

Correct bend at the counter-canter. The horse's neck is turned slightly to the outside and the rider's outside leg is active on the girth keeping the horse straight. The inside rein (now the rein facing the outside of the school) gives flexibly, to enable the horse to engage its hindquarters actively.

counter-canter are a collected, well-engaged canter, as well as the horse's willingness to accept the aids for the canter on both reins. At the counter-canter, the corners of the school are rounded off slightly. In the corner, the rider should turn the horse's forehand early and retain the hindquarters underneath the centre of balance of the horse by resting the outside leg (i.e. the leg which faces the inside of the school) firmly against the horse's side. On the long sides, the posture of the horse is improved again by means of a few half-halts. In the corners and on the short sides, the rider's rein aids should become more flexible, but the forward impulsion should be maintained energetically, in order to prevent the horse from losing balance and falling out. If the horse does lose balance and falls out, the rider should restart the counter-canter again calmly on the long side (possibly on the second track). The horse should not be punished for failing to maintain the correct pace. If the rider's aids are applied correctly and the horse continues to fall out, it probably cannot yet engage its hindlegs and transfer its weight onto the hindquarters sufficiently. Punishing the horse in this case would only lead to resistance and make the exercise more difficult to perform. Instead, the prerequisites for the counter-canter need to be improved.

In order to perform the counter-canter, the rider should initially ride a collected canter on the correct leg and then change the rein at a half-volte out of the corner or diagonally across half of the school. The rider's aids correspond to those of the canter on the inside leg. Shortly after changing the rein, however, he should ride forward with increased impulsion to maintain the engagement of the hindquarters. At the counter-canter he needs to ensure that the horse's posture remains even.

Initially, the things to prevent at the counter-canter are the horse falling apart and not placing its hindlegs sufficiently under the body, as an increased engagement of the hindquarters is nec-

essary here, which will at the same time improve the canter.

The rider must make sure not to bend the horse too far, as this would lead to the hindquarters swinging outwards, which would make the counter-canter unpleasant for the horse. The rider will have to apply his legs with more power. At the counter-canter, the outside leg of the rider will have to become active repeatedly to prevent the hindquarters from falling out and to maintain an active engagement. The rider should ride only short stretches at the counter-canter followed by canter on the inside leg with plenty of impulsion and extension.

Ensuring that the horse remains straight in its vertical axis is important at the counter-canter as well. The forehand of the horse is led slightly to the middle of the school and restrained well with the outside aids. The inside rein (the one on the outside of the school) should continue to give flexibly at each stride so that the horse can use its inside hindleg and place it well under the body.

Transitions from the counter-canter to the walk and to the canter on the inside leg will improve the counter-canter. These exercises help improve the flexibility and responsiveness of the horse and the simple change from the counter-canter to the normal canter in intermediate dressage tests. Here, as in the transitions from the normal canter, the rider should ensure that the back and leg aids prevail and that he does not pull the horse by the reins at any cost. As it is more difficult for the horse to transfer its weight to its hindquarters at the counter-canter, it will take some time until the transition to a slower pace from the counter-canter is as successful as from a normal canter. As always, the voice aid should be used initially as a support. If the rider experiences difficulties, he can start the counter-canter on the second or third track to begin with. He should always avoid bending the horse excessively to the outside.

Once the horse has mastered the counter-canter around the whole school, it should learn to complete a full circle as well. Here, the most difficult thing is to maintain the correct line of the circle, if the rider bends the horse too much to the outside and prevents it from using its inside hindleg to place it further under the body by

not giving the inside rein. The horse should remain on the bit and responsive to the aids at the counter-canter in order to be able to correctly perform dressage movements in the school.

TURN ON THE HAUNCHES AND DEMI-PIROUETTE AT THE WALK

The turn on the haunches is performed from the halt, the demi-pirouette in motion at the walk. In this movement, the horse turns its forehand around the stationary inside hindleg. The rider should ensure that the turning point is as close to the inside hindleg as poss-

The demi-pirouette at the walk is easier to learn than the turn on the haunches from the halt. The process of the movement remains the same. Photo: Ruttmann

The horse is turned in the direction of the movement and bent laterally. The forelegs cross over, the hind-legs make a small circle without crossing over, at a four-beat of the walk. Photograph: Ruttmann

ible. The turn on the haunches is classed as an exercise of collection, as it distinctly improves the horse's willingness to collect. It is the most difficult movement at the intermediary level and is rarely performed completely correctly.

The horse should be bent in the direction of the intended movement and should perform a circle with its forelegs around its hind legs while bent on the lateral axis. The forelegs cross over during this movement, and the hindlegs perform a small circle at the four-beat walk sequence without cross-

ing over. Only at the last step which leads the horse back on the track forwards-sideways, may the hindlegs cross over.

Unlike the turn on the forehand, the horse is not simply turned but also bent. The rider's inside leg acts on the girth to encourage the bend and the outside leg rests one hand's width behind the girth as a restraint and prevents the hindquarters from swinging outwards. The rider's weight is transferred to the inside. The rider should make sure not to bend in the hip.

The rider's outside leg acts as a restraint; it prevents the hindquarters from swinging out. However it must not be applied to drive the horse sideways. Photo: Ruttmann

The inside rein gives the horse the necessary position and can lead the horse slightly sideways. The outside rein describes the limit of the position of the horse's neck but remains flexible enough to maintain the forward impulsion. When riding a demi-pirouette, it is regarded as a more serious fault if the horse steps backwards. As in all movements, the reins are used primarily to maintain contact with the horse's mouth and keep it on the bit.

For this purpose it can give and take and this acts to stop the horse lying on the bit or trying to evade it.

The demi-pirouette at the walk is generally easier to execute than the turn on the haunches from the halt, as the horse moves straight into the turn from the walk and the hind legs are already further underneath the centre of balance and the horse usually moves sideways better. This is particularly true if the demi-pirouette is ridden from the trot. For this purpose, the horse is asked to perform a transition to the walk and then immediately turned into the demi-pirouette. However, for this movement the horse needs to be on the bit, relaxed and responsive.

The turn on the haunches should not look like this. The rider has bent her hip. The horse's head is too low, it twists on its vertical axis and steps out with the hindquarters.

Before initiating the demi-pirouette it is important for the horse to walk correctly responding to the aids. The rider asks the horse for increased impulsion in rhythm to shift the weight closer to the centre of balance and asks for a more intensive contact with the horse's mouth. One horse's length before performing the demi-pirouette, the horse is positioned and bent slightly inwards.

In order to initiate the turn on the haunches, the inexperienced rider can first ride one or two strides forwards during which he starts to bend the

horse to the inside and bends around his legs. Then the inside rein leads the forehand of the horse onto a circle around the hindquarters. Both reins determine the bend of the horse's neck and act as absorbing or relaxing half-halts to allow the sideways movement of the horse.

The rider's inside leg maintains impulsion and the bend of the horse and asks for the hind legs to step in rhythm on the spot. The outside leg prevents the hindquarters from swinging out, which happens if the horse is bent too far to the inside. At the same

The reins maintain the contact to the horse's mouth. The outside rein restrains, the inside rein determines the bend. Unlike in this photograph, the horse should not overbend and the rider should give more with the reins.
Photo: Ruttmann

time, it supports the lifting of the hind legs towards the centre of balance through short impulses. The outside leg may not push the horse sideways as this would encourage the horse to cross over with its hindlegs.

A useful preliminary exercise to performing the turn on the haunches is the riding of very small voltes (between five and six metres diameter) at the walk. This makesthe horse more supple and it learns to find its balance when it is bent laterally. The rider can then initiate a turn on the haunches from a volte.

The rider needs to maintain the bend created by the volte. As before, the forehand moves in a circle. The hind legs, on the other hand, perform a small circle, restricted by the rider's aids. The rider can now change repeatedly between a volte and a turn on the haunches in the centre of the school in order to maintain the motion and impulsion of the horse. Another exercise which may prove useful is to initially ride the turn on the haunches in the centre of the circle and, if necessary, ask for more than a 180-degree turn with pauses in between. However, the

The turn on the haunches is terminated at the halt, the demi-pirouette from the walk in motion.

horse should never be expected to do too much, so it does not begin to resist the rider.

Performing the turn on the haunches requires a certain amount of collection from the horse. During the turn the horse needs to actively engage its hindquarters and raise its head and shoulders. It should not however be allowed to evade rounding its back. The increased flexion of the hocks and fetlock joints will facilitate the execution of the turn on the haunches and the horse will be able to perform this movement with panache.

One commonly occurring fault of the turn on the haunches is that of the

horse leading with the hindquarters into the turn. In this case, the rider has failed to turn the forehand of the horse inwards before beginning the turn on the haunches. This way, the horse is not asked to complete the turn within four or five steps but will instead need to take far more steps. The rider should turn the forehand around more, similar to riding the volte.

Often the turn on the haunches becomes far too large because the horse turns its hindquarters on too large a circle. In most cases, the hind-legs also cross over. In this case, the rider needs to ensure not to push the horse side-

Perfect free walk on a long rein. The horse's topline is rounded and it walks forwards with plenty of impulsion, stretching its neck and head forward and downwards in response to the rider's rein aids.

ways with his outside leg and to bend the horse more, as well as making sure that the turn is not planned forwards too much.

If the horse fails to bend laterally, the turn on the haunches looks more like leg-yielding on the spot. The rider's inside leg needs to have greater influence to bend the horse and at the same time the turn needs to be made smaller by leading the forehand around on a smaller circle.

However, the rider has to take note whether the horse is already physically able to balance itself in smaller turns. He can find this out by riding a small volte at the walk whereby the horse should be able to balance without a problem. A very serious fault is the incorrect bend to the outside during the turn on the haunches, as this prevents the horse from bending laterally. Usually in this case, the horse will hurry the turn. The rider can prevent this from happening by restricting the sideways movement of the horse with his restraining rein aid and inside leg. For practice purposes the turn on the haunches should only be ridden one or two steps at the time, before asking the horse to come back down on the bit. At the same time, the lateral position and bend need to be improved by riding voltes.

WALKING ON A LONG REIN

When walking on a long rein the horse should willingly stretch forward and downwards through lengthening the rein. Contact should be maintained throughout. The horse should stretch until its mouth is about level with the forearm joint. It should chew willingly on the bit the entire time. Throughout, the horse should not lose its balance.

If the movement "Walking on a long rein" is required in a dressage test, the judges want to know whether the horse has been ridden correctly from behind, responding to the aids, and therefore willingly stretching itself when the reins are lengthened. At the same time, it needs to maintain the same rhythm and tempo. It must under no circumstances ignore the back and seat aids of the rider and run off. "Walking on the long rein" is also a good practice exercise as it strengthens the trust between the horse and the rider's hands and gives the horse a welcome break from the strenuous upright posture at the normal paces. The change between stretching the neck forward and downwards and maintaining an upright posture also strengthens the neck muscles better than riding the horse in the stretched position all the time, as the latter would encourage it to fall onto the forehand.

In order to achieve a satisfactory result, the exercise needs to be executed properly. The rider should drive the horse forwards energetically at the working tempo to encourage it to stretch its neck forward and down-

wards. If the horse gently pulls in the right direction, the rider gives the reins bit by bit. He must make sure, however, not to lose contact with the horse's mouth. The contact should be maintained in the same way as when the horse is normally on the bit. The rider is just as able to give and take with a longer rein as with a short rein. The horse remains responsive to the rider's back and leg aids and maintains the rhythm and tempo of the pace. If the horse tends to start hurrying, the rider will have to shorten the rein repeatedly, bring back the horse to the original tempo and then start lengthening the reins once again. In time the horse will learn not to exploit the giving of the reins immediately but will remain responsive to the rider's aids. Then, the reins can be lengthened further.

GIVE AND RETAKE REINS FOR A FEW STRIDES WITHOUT CHANGE OF TEMPO

When giving and retaking the reins for a few strides at the trot or canter, the rider momentarily relinquishes the contact for two to three horse's lengths and pushes both hands forward along the crest of the mane. The horse has to maintain the correct posture and remain responsive to the aids and on the bit. It does not count as a fault, if the line from the forehead to the nose moves slightly in front of the vertical, as long as the horse remains on the bit.

During training the rider should also check the posture of the horse from time to time by giving the reins for a few strides. This way he can determine how well the horse is reacting to his weight and leg aids and whether it is going forward freely independent of the rein.

To practise this exercise, giving and retaking the reins is also carried out in turns and circles with just one hand. In this case, the rider gives the inside rein to check how well the horse is responding on the outside rein. This exercise, however, should not be carried out all the time, leading to the rider riding with looped reins and thereby relinquishing the even contact with the horse's mouth.

JUMPING

Naturally, all rules regarding the aids also apply for jumping. The daily training of the horse to keep it supple, relaxed and responsive and to improve the paces, needs to be applied to the showjumper or event horse in the same way as to the dressage horse. For jumping, however, the focus in on the canter. For the forward seat, the stirrups are shortened by two to three holes. The angle of the rider's legs becomes more acute, although the forwards – and sideways – driving leg aids come into effect at the same height. The weight aids are also transferred to the horse's back via the seat bones. However, the rider's seat is less upright. Depending on the degree of

Forward seat with relatively long stirrups. The rider remains over the centre of balance of the horse with balanced upper body. The hands holding the reins can be placed on both sides of the neck. Photo: Schmidt-Neuhaus

forwardness of the seat, the spine tips forward. If the buttocks are lifted off the saddle in the extreme position, the rider transfers his weight aids to the horse via his thighs.

When approaching the jump, it is necessary to keep the horse gently on the bit via the back with half-halts. The rider influences the length of the stride at the canter and gallop through his seat, by driving the horse forwards energetically with his hips or slowing down the movement. The length of the stride at the canter is important in order to get the jump-off right, i.e. the take-off point of the horse must be at the right distance in front of the jump. At the moment of take-off the rider gives a distinct aid by pressing against the horse's sides with both legs. The horse reacts to this and jumps. A well-ridden horse waits for this signal from the rider. Over the fence at the moment of suspension, the legs remain closed around the horse's sides. The

rider thus strengthens his seat in order to be able to balance his weight over the fence, and the horse is encouraged to pull up its legs in order to take the jump without a fault.

Before take-off, the reins are held with even pressure. At the moment of take-off the rider goes forwards gently with both hands and allows the horse to stretch to its full extent. The giving of the rein allows the horse to maintain its own balance sufficiently and to round its back in the correct bascule. During the landing phase the reins are gently taken up again.

The rapid communication between rider and horse is of particular importance when jumping. For this purpose, the horse needs to be exercised daily and needs to practise the prompt and correct reaction to the lightest aids. This will allow the rider to jump a course faultlessly and in the shortest time possible.

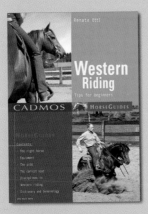

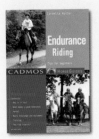

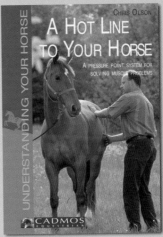

OTHER CADMOS BOOKS

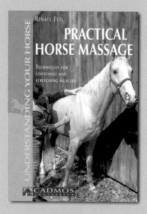